I'm Reading About

MAINE

The Pine Tr[illegible]e!

GALLOPADE

by Carole Marsh

Printed and Manufactured in Peachtree City, GA., USA
www.gallopade.com

Book design: John Hanson

Editorial manager: Janice Baker

Maine is a great state.
It is one of a kind.

What makes Maine special?
Let's read about it
and see!

NATIVE AMERICANS

Who lived in Maine first?

Native Americans did!

They moved around to find food.
They hunted in Maine's woods.
They fished in Maine's rivers.
They gathered fruits and seeds and nuts.

EXPLORERS

The first explorers came to Maine in 1524.
They came from the country of France.

Giovanni da Verrazzano was their leader.
He and his men were exploring new land!

SETTLEMENT

A group of people came from England to America.
They started the first settlement in Maine.
The colonists built a fort and named it
Fort St. George.
The colony became known as Popham Colony.

The colonists left Popham
Colony after one year.
They returned to England.

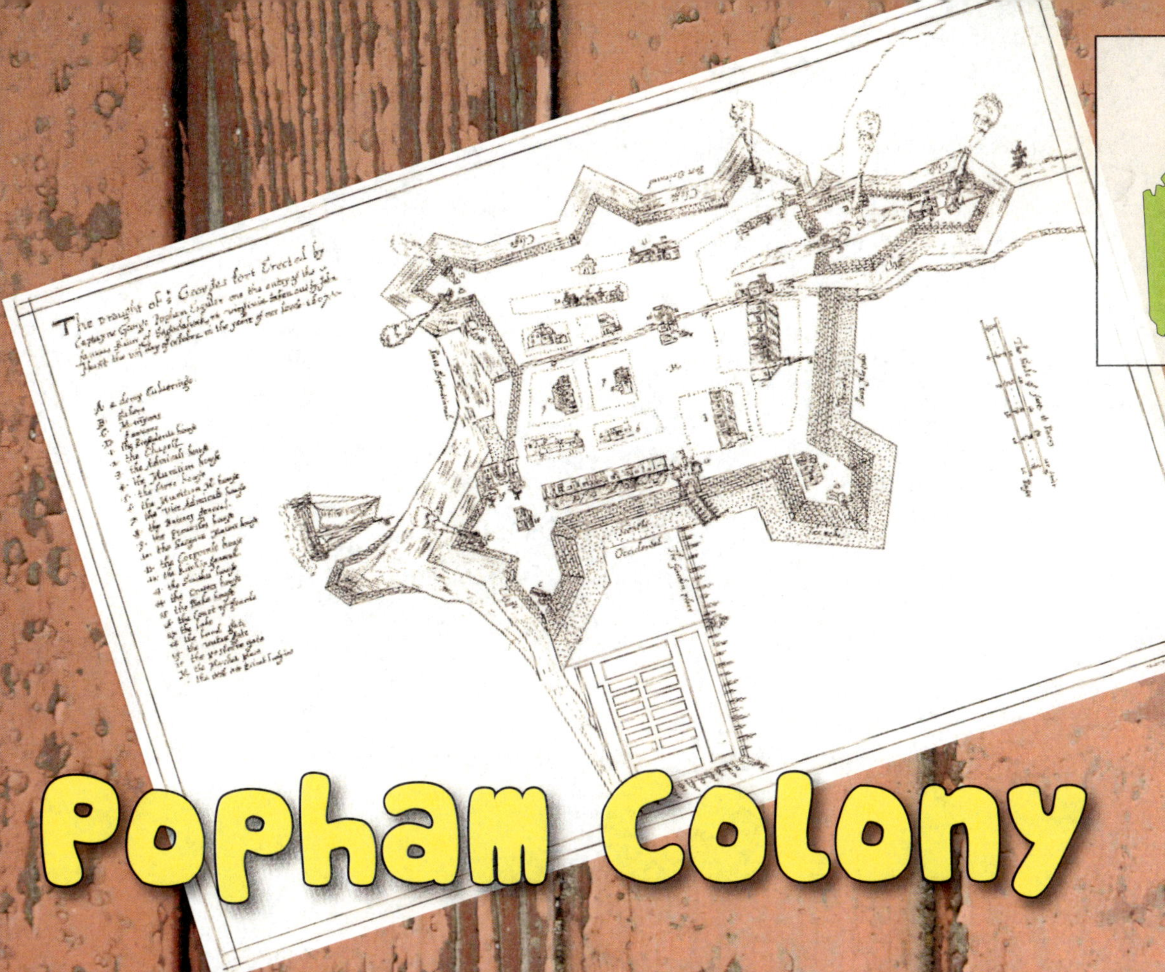

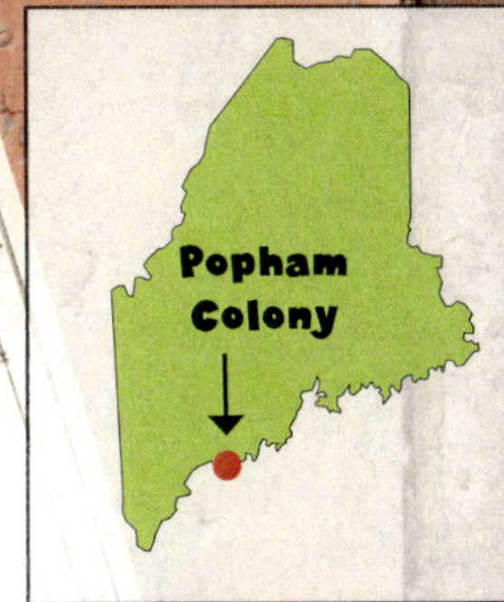

Popham Colony

STATEHOOD

Maine was the 23rd state
to join the United States of America!

Isn't it great,
to be a state!
I bet Maine
could hardly wait!

Maine became a state in 1820.

Maine
The 23rd State

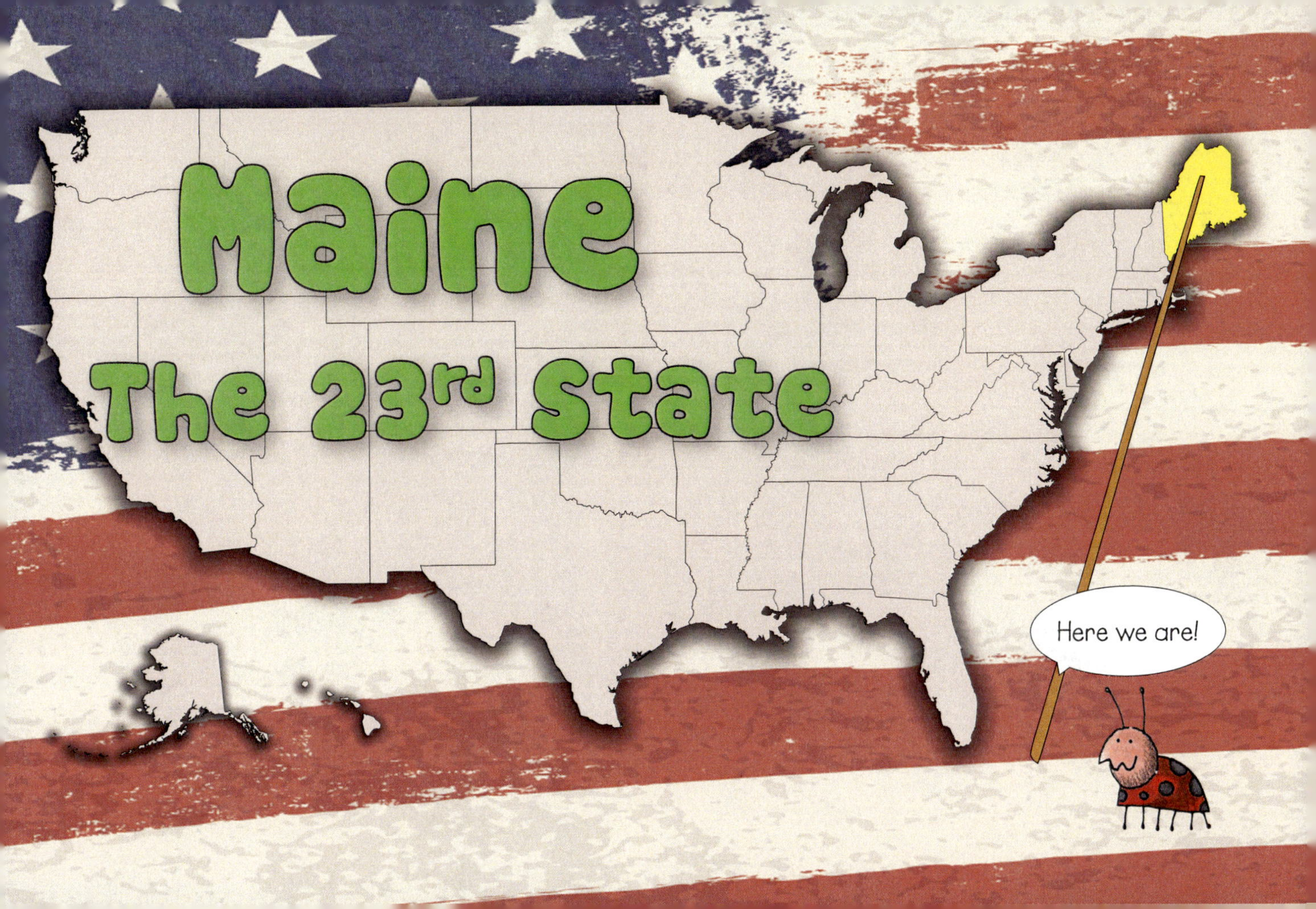

FLAG

I am the state flag.
I was adopted in 1909.

What color am I?
I am blue.

Look at me.
What else do you see?

I fly high over the state of Maine!

DIRIGO
MAINE

CAPITAL

Say hello to Augusta,
the capital city of Maine!

There is an important building in Augusta.
It is the State House.
Maine's laws are made there!

State House
Augusta
Capital

SEAL

I am a seal,
but I am not the State Seal.
If I were, I would be very important.
I would be stamped on many official papers.
(Ouch, that might hurt!)

DIRIGO
MAINE

Now, that's official!

NICKNAME

State nicknames are fun!
State nicknames are great!
They share fun facts
about each state!

Maine's nickname is "The Pine Tree State."

Forests cover almost 90 percent of Maine!

The Pine Tree State

BORDERS

Look at Maine.
Maine is in a region called "the Northeast."

Maine borders one other state.
It also borders the country of Canada.
Find Maine and its neighbors on the map!

Borders

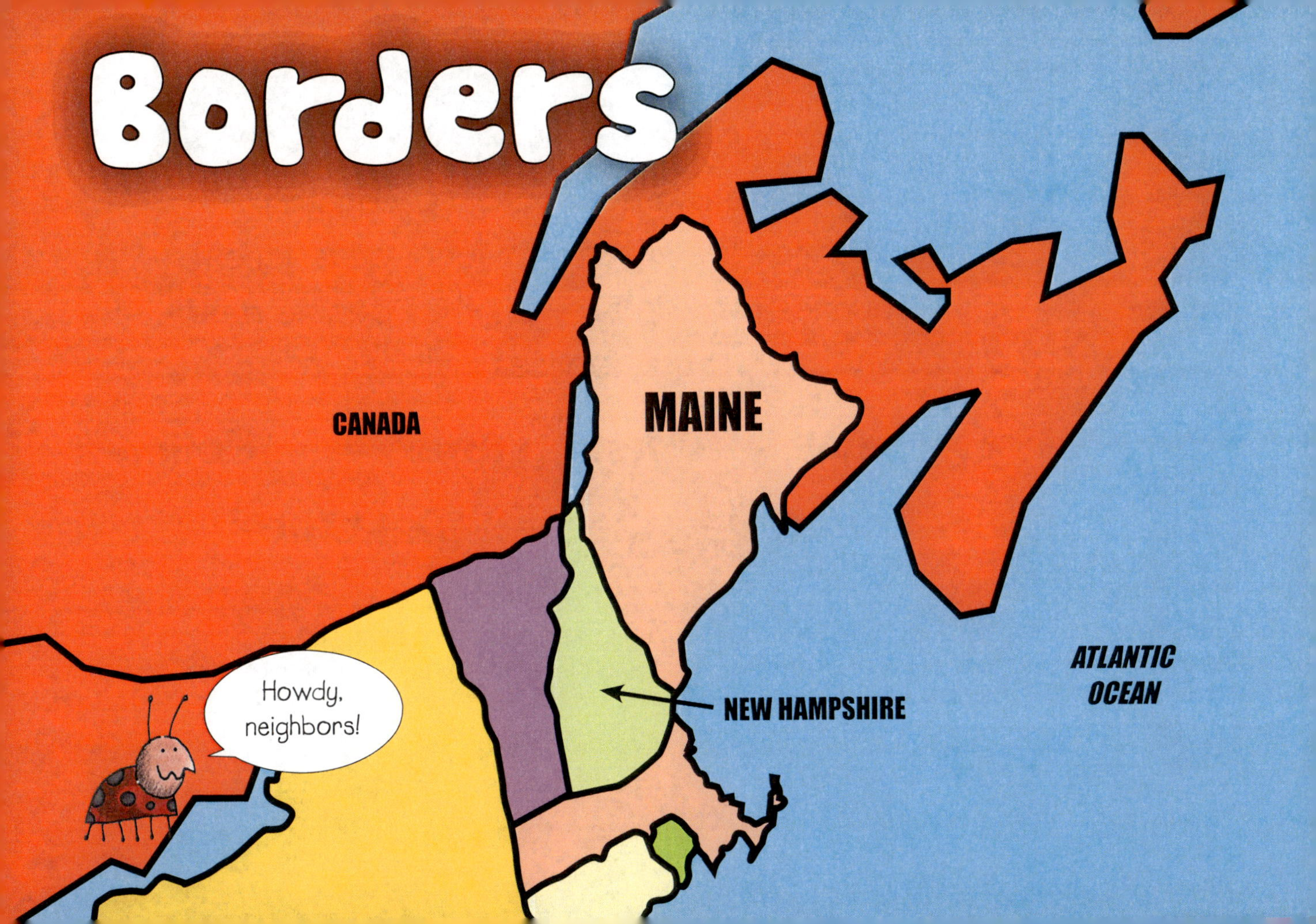
CANADA
MAINE
NEW HAMPSHIRE
ATLANTIC OCEAN
Howdy, neighbors!

COUNTIES

Maine is divided into 16 counties.
Counties are a form of local government.
Counties provide services that people need!
Those services include:

Schools **Parks** **Libraries** **Police**

Firefighters **and More!**

Counties

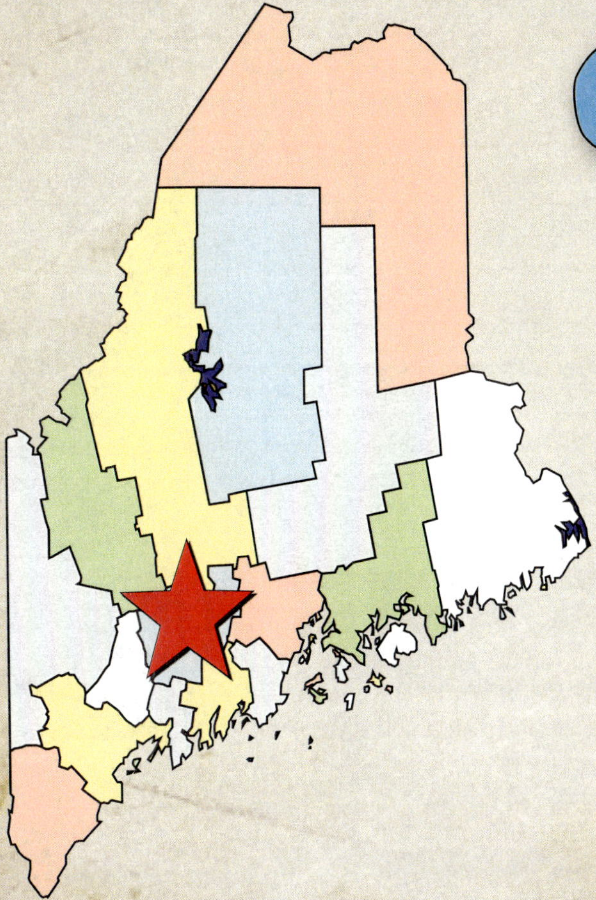

MAINE'S CAPITAL, AUGUSTA, IS IN KENNEBEC COUNTY.

PEOPLE

Many famous people

Henry Wadsworth Longfellow

Poet whose works include "Paul Revere's Ride"

Milton Bradley

Founded the Milton Bradley Company, famous for board games

Louis Sockalexis

One of the first Native Americans to play Major League Baseball

call our state home!

E.B. White

Author who wrote *Charlotte's Web* and *Stuart Little*

Margaret Chase Smith

First woman to serve in both houses of the U.S. Congress

Joan Benoit

First woman to win an Olympic marathon

PEOPLE

Chickadee

BIRD

I am the state bird, and I fly
over Maine, proud and high.

As I fly, up in the sky,
I flap my wings to tell you "Hi!"

The Maine state bird is the Chickadee.

White Pine Cone and Tassel

FLOWER

I am the White Pine Cone and Tassel.
I am the state flower.

I grow where it's mild and sunny.
I look like a brown cone with woody petals.
I help make Maine beautiful!

Look at me! Smell me!
I am a different kind of flower.
I am unique!

White Pine

TREE

I am a White Pine—I'm the state tree.
All over Maine is where to find me.

My roots run deep, they keep me strong.
My needles stay green, all year long.

I stand up straight, big and tall.
Don't climb too high—it would hurt to fall!

Honeybee

I am the Honeybee.
I am the state insect.

I might sting you if you bother me.
But really, I am your friend.

I carry pollen from flower to flower.
I make honey.
I help Maine crops grow.

BZZZZZZZZZZZZ!

INSECT

Atlantic Ocean

BEACHES

Let's go to the beach!

We can swim in the waves.
We can play in the sand.

We can build a big castle
where water meets land.

Maine's beaches are home to many animals:

Lobster **Fish** **Birds** **Crabs** **Dolphins** **and More!**

Mountains

MOUNTAINS

Maine's mountains are the place to be.
Hiking, fishing, camping—
fun for you and me.

Winter weather brings lots of snow.
Temperatures drop to freezing and below!

Rivers

RIVERS

Maine has many rivers.
People like to use rivers for boating and fishing!

This habitat is home to many animals:

Birds Deer Snakes Frogs Fish and More!

The Kennebec River flows completely within the state of Maine.

Portland Head Light

LANDMARK

There are many lighthouses along the coast of Maine! The Portland Head Light is the oldest one.

A lighthouse is a tower with a large light at the top. Lighthouses help guide boats safely to shore.

The Portland Head Light is still used today. The original light was a huge lamp filled with whale oil!

Maine Products

AGRICULTURE

Maine has many farms.
Why?
Because Maine has good soil and a mild climate!

Some of the top products from Maine are:

Potatoes **Blueberries** **Apples** **Maple Syrup**

Sports in Maine

SPORTS

Baseball! Basketball! Hockey! Football!
Maine has it all.

Whether you like to watch or play,
You are sure to have a ball!

Black Bears **Huskies**

Polar Bears

& More!

Maine: Home of Lobsters

CLAIM TO FAME

Maine is known for delicious lobsters!
Many lobsters live in the waters off the coast of Maine.
Lobster fishing is an important business in Maine.
People across America love to eat Maine lobsters!

Lobsters can move forward, backward, and sideways!

GLOSSARY

climate: weather conditions in an area over a long period of time

colony: a settlement ruled by another country

habitat: a place where plants or animals naturally live

laws: rules made by the government

marathon: a long run just over 26 miles in length

original: first, or earliest

pollen: a yellow powder that helps plants make new plants

region: an area that has similar characteristics

settlement: the first community in an area

unique: something that is the only one of its kind